jellyphants and woolly jumpers

Amanda Li is a children's writer and editor.
She lives in London with her two daughters, Isabelle
and Millie, who are both brilliant joke-tellers.

Jane Eccles lives in Hampshire with her husband,
Graham, and son, Theo and Celeste the cat.

jellyphants and woolly jumpers

my first joke book

Compiled by Amanda Li

Illustrated by Jane Eccles

MACMILLAN CHILDREN'S BOOKS

First published 2006 by Macmillan Children's Books
a division of Macmillan Publishers Limited
20 New Wharf Road, London N1 9RR
Basingstoke and Oxford
Associated companies throughout the world
www.panmacmillan.com

ISBN 978-0-330-44151-3

17 19 18 16

A CIP catalogue record for this book is available from
the British Library.

Printed and bound in the UK by CPI Group (UK), Croydon, CR0 4YY

For Millie Yates and Oisin Bracken

What's grey and wobbly?

A jellyphant.

What do you call a donkey
with three legs?
A wonkey.

Where do baby apes sleep?
In apricots.

What do you get if you sit
under a cow?
A pat on the head.

What is a crocodile's favourite card game?
Snap!

Why should you never play games in the jungle?
Because there are a lot of cheetahs about.

What do birds need when they are sick?
Tweetment!

How does a pig get to hospital?
In a hambulance.

What's a camel's favourite
party game?
Musical Humps.

What's a cow's favourite
party game?
Moosical Chairs.

Why are elephants so wrinkled?
Have you ever tried ironing one?

What's black and white and red all over?
A zebra with sunburn.

How do you catch
a squirrel?
Climb up a tree and act like
a nut.

What do birds say at
Halloween?
'Trick or tweet!'

How do you keep a skunk
from smelling?
Hold its nose.

What do you call a cow
eating grass?
A lawn mooer.

What do you call a sleepy Stegosaurus?
A Stegosnorus.

What do you call a dinosaur with one eye?
A 'Doyouthinkhesaurus'.

What do you call a wet dinosaur?
A Driplodocus.

What do you call a T-rex with a banana in each ear?
Anything you like - it can't hear you!

Why did the man buy all the birds at the pet shop?
They were going cheep.

What kind of pet makes
the loudest noise?
A trum-pet.

What do you call a cat
with eight legs?
An octopuss.

What kind of stories
do cats like?
Furry tales.

Why don't dogs drive cars?
They can never find a
barking space.

What happened to the cat who swallowed a ball of wool?
She had mittens.

woof!

What do dogs and trees have in common?
Bark!

What kind of dog smells of onions?
A hot dog.

What do you call a rabbit with fleas?
Bugs Bunny.

What do rabbits sing at birthday parties?
'Hoppy birthday to you...'

What does a mouse put in its drink?

Mice cubes.

What's a mouse's
favourite game?
Hide and Squeak.

What pet is always smiling?
A grinny pig.

Where do you find a
tortoise with no legs?
Where you left it.

What did one slug say
to the other?
'See you next slime!'

What do you call
an evil insect?
A baddy-long-legs.

What did one bee
say to the other?
'Buzz off!'

What is the largest kind of ant?
A gi-ant.

What's black and yellow and goes 'zub, zub'?
A bee flying backwards.

Where do you take a sick wasp?
To the waspital.

WASPITAL

What goes 'hiss swish, hiss swish'?
A windscreen viper.

Why can't you play jokes on snakes?

Because you can never pull their legs.

What do snakes learn at school?

Hiss-tory.

What goes '99 bonk,
99 bonk'?
A centipede with
a wooden leg.

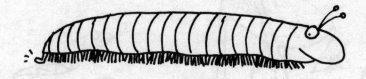

Why couldn't the centipede
be in the football team?
He took too long to put his
boots on.

Why did the fly fly?
Because the spider spied 'er.

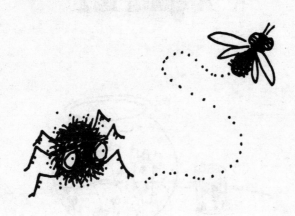

What is the difference between a fly and a bird?
A bird can fly but a fly can't bird.

What fish is the most valuable?
A goldfish.

What fish goes well with ice cream?
A jellyfish.

What fish only swims at night?
A starfish.

What is a knight's favourite fish?
A swordfish.

Why are fish no good at tennis?
They don't like to get too close to the net.

Why did the lobster blush?
Because the sea weed!

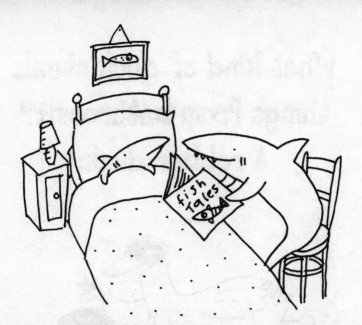

What do sharks read before they go to sleep?
A bite-time story.

How do you cut through the ocean?
With a sea saw.

What kind of duck steals
things from bathrooms?
A robber duck.

What did the duck
say to the waiter?
'Put it on my bill, please.'

What do you get if
you cross a frog
with a fizzy drink?
Croak-a-Cola.

Where do frogs keep
their money?
In a river bank.

Where do frogs hang their coats?
In the croakroom.

What does a frog eat with a burger?
French flies.

What do witches wrap presents with?
Spellotape.

What do you call a witch made of sand?
A sandwich!

Why do witches all look the same?
So you can't tell which witch is which.

What goes
'Cackle, cackle, bonk!'?
A witch laughing her head off.

How do you make
a witch itch?
Take away her 'w'.

What do witches use
in the summer?
Suntan potion.

How do ghosts travel around?
By scaroplane.

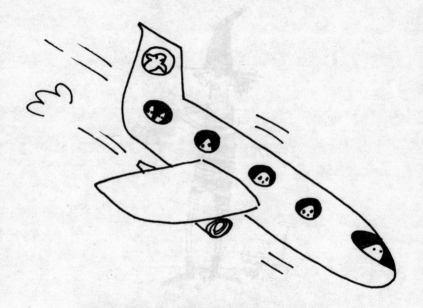

Where do ghosts buy stamps?
At the ghost office.

What do ghosts do before
they go to sleep?
Read a fright-time story.

What do ghosts eat
for dinner?
Spookhetti.

What game do baby ghosts like to play?
Hide and Eek!

How do ghosts like their eggs?
Terror-fried.

On what day do
monsters eat people?
Chews-day.

Where does a big scary
monster sit on the train?
Anywhere he likes!

What would you say if you met a monster with three heads?
'Hello, hello, hello!'

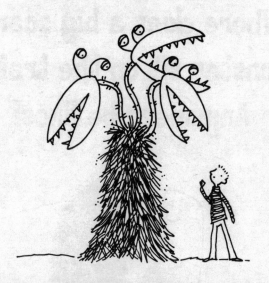

What's big, scary and goes up and down?
A monster on a trampoline.

What do you call a skeleton that stays in bed all day?
Lazybones.

Why didn't the skeleton go to the ball?
He had no body to go with.

How do skeletons get in
touch with each other?
On the tele-bone.

How do you know if a baby
skeleton's in the room?
You can hear its rattle.

What do frogs eat for breakfast?
Coco Hops.

What do cats eat for breakfast?
Mice Krispies.

What do birds eat for breakfast?
Tweetabix.

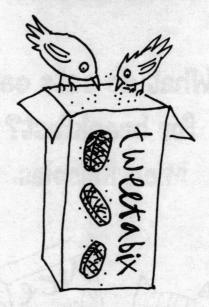

What do snowmen eat for breakfast?
Snowflakes.

What's a sea monster's
favourite meal?
Fish and ships.

What swings through
the trees and tastes
good with milk?
A chocolate chimp cookie.

What colour is a burp?
Burple.

Why did the jelly wobble?
It saw the milk shake.

What vegetable is
always wet?
A leek.

What do you call two
bananas?
A pair of slippers.

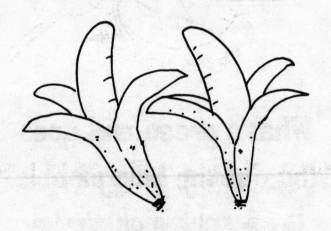

What's the fastest vegetable?
A runner bean.

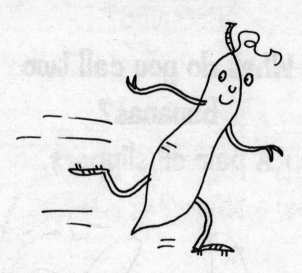

What's green and goes 'boing, boing'?
A spring onion.

Knock, knock!
Who's there?
Boo.
Boo who?
Don't cry, it's only a joke!

Knock, knock!
Who's there?
Luke.
Luke who?
Luke out, there's
a monster
behind you!

Knock, knock! Who's there?
Ivor. Ivor who?
Ivor great idea.

Knock, knock! Who's there?
Nose. Nose who?
I nose a lot of jokes, I do.

Knock, knock! Who's there?
Noise. Noise who?
Noise to meet you.

Knock, knock! Who's there?
Kanga. Kanga who?
No, kangaROO.

Knock, knock! Who's there?
Hatch. Hatch who?
Bless you!

Knock, knock! Who's there?
Ants. Ants who?
Ants in your pants!

Why is Cinderella so
bad at football?
She always runs away
from the ball.

What's a spider's
favourite fairy tale?
Spinderella.

Which fairy is the smelliest?
Stinkerbell.

What kind of pet did Aladdin have?
A flying car-pet.

How does Jack Frost get to work?
By icicle.

Who flies through the air in his underwear?
Peter Pants.

What does Tarzan sing at Christmas?
'Jungle Bells, Jungle Bells...'

Who shouted 'Knickers!' at the Big Bad Wolf?
Little Rude Riding Hood.

How do you start
a teddy bear race?
Say 'Ready, teddy, go!'

What do farmers use to add
their numbers?
A cowculator.

Why was the number six sad?
Because seven eight nine.

Why did the boy take his pencil to bed?
He wanted to draw the curtains.

Why did the boy throw butter out of the window? Because he wanted to see a butter fly.

What flies and is wobbly? A jellycopter.

What do you call a
snowman in the desert?
A puddle.

What do traffic wardens
have in their sandwiches?
Traffic jam.

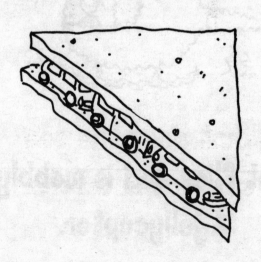

What did one traffic light say to the other?
'Don't look, I'm changing.'

What does the sea say to the sand?
Nothing, it just waves.

What did the stamp say to the envelope?
'Stick with me and we'll go places.'

What did one octopus say to the other octopus?
'I want to hold your hand, hand, hand, hand, hand, hand, hand, hand.'

What goes up when the rain
comes down?
An umbrella.

What gets wetter the more
it dries?
A towel.

What kind of puzzle makes you angry?
A crossword.

What kind of bow is impossible to tie?
A rainbow.

What room has got no floor,
ceiling or door?
A mushroom.

What keys are furry?
Monkeys.

Why did the orange have a day off school?
It wasn't peeling very well.

Do cows cheat in tests?
Yes, they copy off each udder.

How do ghosts get to school?

On a ghoul bus.

Why did the computer squeak?

Somebody stepped on its mouse.

Why didn't the nose make the school football team? It wasn't picked.

Teacher: If I had twenty bananas in one hand and thirty bananas in the other hand, what would I have?

Pupil: Er, very big hands?

What do you get if you
cross a pudding with
a cowpat?
A smelly jelly.

What do you get if you
cross a bear with a fridge?
A teddy brrrrr.

What do you get if you cross a sheep with a kangaroo?
A woolly jumper.

What do you get if you cross a dog with a cockerel?
A cock-a-poodle-doo!

Doctor, doctor, nobody listens to me!
Next, please!

Doctor, doctor, I keep thinking I'm a dustbin!
Oh, stop talking rubbish.

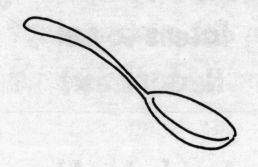

Doctor, doctor,
I keep thinking I'm a spoon!
Just sit down and don't stir.

Doctor, doctor, I keep
thinking I'm a pair
of curtains!
Oh, pull yourself together.

**Waiter, what's this
fly doing in my soup?
It looks like it's learning
to swim, sir.**

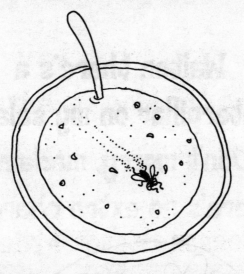

**Waiter, there's a frog
in my soup!
I'll tell him to hop it.**

Waiter, there's a
fly in my soup!
Don't shout, madam, or
everyone will want one.

Waiter, there's a
caterpillar on my salad!
Don't worry, madam,
there's no extra charge.